MISSOURI

Natasha Evdokimoff

AV² provides enriched content that supplements and complements this book. Weigl's AV² books strive to create inspired learning and engage young minds in a total learning experience.

Your AV² Media Enhanced books come alive with...

Audio
Listen to sections of the book read aloud.

Key Words
Study vocabulary, and complete a matching word activity.

Video
Watch informative video clips.

Quizzes
Test your knowledge.

Embedded Weblinks
Gain additional information for research.

Slide Show
View images and captions, and prepare a presentation.

Try This!
Complete activities and hands-on experiments.

... and much, much more!

Go to **www.av2books.com,** and enter this book's unique code.

BOOK CODE

P 5 2 5 4 9 6

AV² by Weigl brings you media enhanced books that support active learning.

Published by AV² by Weigl
350 5th Avenue, 59th Floor
New York, NY 10118
Website: www.av2books.com

Library of Congress Cataloging-in-Publication Data
Names: Evdokimoff, Natasha, author.
Title: Missouri : the Show Me State / Natasha Evdokimoff.
Description: New York, NY : AV2 by Weigl, 2016. | Series: Discover America |
  Includes bibliographical references and index.
Identifiers: LCCN 2015047987 (print) | LCCN 2015049097 (ebook) | ISBN
  9781489648907 (hard cover : alk. paper) | ISBN 9781489648914 (soft cover :
  alk. paper) | ISBN 9781489648921 (Multi-User eBook)
Subjects: LCSH: Missouri--Juvenile literature.
Classification: LCC F466.3 .E946 2016 (print) | LCC F466.3 (ebook) | DDC 977.8--dc23
LC record available at http://lccn.loc.gov/2015047987

Printed in the United States of America, in Brainerd, Minnesota
1 2 3 4 5 6 7 8 9 20 19 18 17 16

042016
220416

Project Coordinator Heather Kissock
Art Director Terry Paulhus

Photo Credits
Every reasonable effort has been made to trace ownership and to obtain permission to reprint copyright material. The publisher would be pleased to have any errors or omissions brought to their attention so that they may be corrected in subsequent printings. The publisher acknowledges Getty Images, Corbis Images, and Alamy as its primary image suppliers for this title.

MISSOURI

Contents

STATE ANIMAL
Missouri Mule

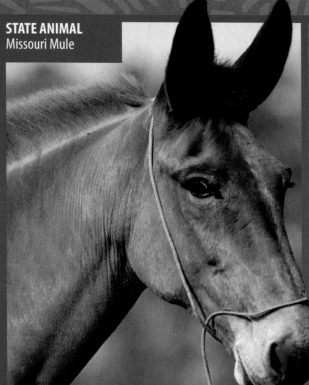

STATE BIRD
Bluebird

STATE TREE
Flowering Dogwood

STATE FLOWER
White Hawthorn

STATE FLAG
Missouri

STATE SEAL
Missouri

Nickname
The Show Me State

Song
"Missouri Waltz," words by J. R. Shannon, music by John Valentine Eppel, and arrangement by Frederick Knight Logan

Entered the Union
February 14, 1859, as the 33rd State

Motto
Salus Populi Suprema Lex Esto
(Let the welfare of the people be the supreme law)

Population
(2010 Census) 5,988,927
Ranked 18th state

Capital
Jefferson City

Discover Missouri

In Missouri, the eastern forests meet the western prairies. North of the Missouri River are gently rolling hills and **fertile** plains. Much of the land south of the river lies in the Ozark Mountains. In the southeastern part of the state, there is a low-lying plain that drains into the Mississippi River.

Missouri has characteristics of several regions of the United States. Its cornfields are reminders of the Midwest, while its cotton fields reflect the South. Missouri's cattle ranches are a fond reminder of the West, and the state's factories recall those found in the East. In politics, Missouri is sometimes referred to as a "swing state," and it often votes for the winner in presidential elections.

With 87 state parks and historic sites, it is easy to experience Missouri outdoors. Visitors can explore the Katy Trail, the longest trail converted from railroad tracks in the nation. Hunting, fishing, and ziplining are also all available in the state.

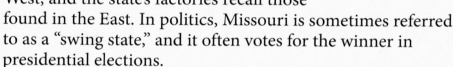

The **confluence** of the Mississippi and Missouri Rivers, near St. Louis, has been a crossroads of North America since Native Americans ruled the land. Today, Missouri also has nearly 125,000 miles of public roads binding the state together. St. Louis and Kansas City have the state's main public airports. Missouri is also a rail center, crisscrossed by many miles of tracks. Passenger trains run between St. Louis and Kansas City.

The Land

The Lewis and Clark Trail Head Plaza, in Jefferson City, sits next to the capitol. The monument commemorates June 4, 1804, when the Lewis and Clark Expedition camped in the area.

Flowing **2,540 miles** from the Rocky Mountains to the Mississippi River, the **Missouri** is the longest river in North America.

The **ST. FRANCIS MOUNTAINS**, in southeast Missouri, are more than **1 BILLION YEARS OLD** and are known for their lead mines.

Lewis and Clark were appointed by President Thomas Jefferson to go explore the west. The two explorers traveled down the Missouri River at the start of their journey.

Beginnings

Missouri gets its name from the river that flows through it. The river is named for a group of Native Americans and may mean "people having canoes." Three main groups, the Illinois, Missouria, and Osage, lived in the area prior to European arrival. The French were the first Europeans to encounter these Native American groups in 1673.

Missouri was the starting point for many journeys westward. In 1804, the explorers Meriwether Lewis and William Clark began their voyage of discovery near St. Louis. The Lewis and Clark Expedition led the way for American trade and settlement in the West.

Until 1845, Missouri was the nation's westernmost state and was known as the Gateway to the West. Many pioneers traveled through Missouri on their way to California, Oregon, and other areas in the West. From Independence, Missouri, just east of Kansas City, settlers and traders could catch the Santa Fe and Oregon trails. Thousands of people who headed west followed these trails before railroads were built.

Where is
MISSOURI?

No state shares more borders with other states than Missouri. Arkansas is to the south, and Oklahoma, Kansas, and Nebraska are to the west. Iowa is to the north, and to the east, across the Mississippi River, are Illinois, Kentucky, and Tennessee.

KANSAS

United States Map

Missouri

Alaska   Hawai'i

MAP LEGEND
- ▦ Missouri
- ☆ Capital City
- ● Major City
- ▪ Mark Twain National Forest
- ▲ Taum Sauk Mountain
- ▫ Bordering States

N

SCALE 0 _____ 50 miles

OKLAHOMA

1 Jefferson City

Jefferson City was founded when Missouri became a state. It was named after Thomas Jefferson and was planned by Daniel M. Boone, son of the famed frontiersman Daniel Boone. Today, more than 40,000 people make Jefferson City their home.

2 Springfield

Founded in 1892, Springfield is Missouri's third-largest city, after Kansas City and St. Louis, and a bustling college town. Missouri State University was founded in Springfield in 1905. Historically, both pioneers and relocated Native Americans passed through or near Springfield.

IOWA

ILLINOIS

MISSOURI

3

★ Jefferson City

1

4

2

● Springfield

ARKANSAS

3 Mark Twain National Forest

The Mark Twain National Forest is a 2,330-square-mile area in southern Missouri that was named after one of the state's most famous residents. The park boasts more than 1.5 million acres of forest, 750 miles of trails, 350 miles of streams, and is home to a wide array of songbirds and other wildlife.

4 Taum Sauk Mountain

At 1,772 feet, Taum Sauk Mountain is the highest point in Missouri. It is the culminating peak of the St. Francis Mountains. The mountain's name has Native American origins, with *Sauk* perhaps meaning "outlet." Nearby is the Mina Sauk Falls, one of the tallest waterfalls in Missouri.

Land Features

Missouri's landscape is a combination of rolling hills, deep valleys, lush forests, and flat farmland. The state's most important natural regions are the Central Lowland in the north, the Ozark Plateau in the south, and the Gulf Coastal Plain in the southeast. The north features gently rolling hills. In the south, especially near the Ozark Mountains, is a rougher landscape.

There are some worn-down mountains in the south that reach no higher than 1,772 feet above sea level. Although not high compared to other ranges, they create a beautiful contrast to the rest of the state. The New Madrid Fault in the southeast produced severe earthquakes in 1811 and 1812. The fault zigzags across the states of Missouri, Arkansas, Tennessee, and Kentucky for 125 miles.

Mississippi River

The Mississippi River is the largest river, in terms of water volume in North America. It begins in Minnesota, and empties into the Gulf of Mexico about 2,340 miles to the south. As the Mississippi flows south past Missouri, both the Missouri and the Ohio Rivers flow into it, making it very wide.

Forests

Forests grow in the hills south of the Missouri River. Missouri has more than 14 million acres of forest land, which include 70 different kinds of trees and shrubs.

Rich Farmland

Northern Missouri has rich soil and good drainage into rivers. These conditions make for excellent farmland.

Onandaga Cave

Missouri boasts more than 6,300 caves. Most of these are found in the Ozark Mountains, south of the Missouri River. Onandaga Cave in Leasburg has been the site of a state park since 1982.

Climate

The weather in Missouri is highly changeable. Temperatures often top 100° Fahrenheit in summer heat waves, and winter can bring low temperatures below 0°F. In winter, the northwest is quite a bit colder than the southeast, but summer temperatures are about the same throughout the state. Summer humidity is high, and rain in the summer comes mostly from drenching thunderstorms. Tornadoes also occur in spring and summer. Precipitation ranges from 34 inches per year in the northwest to 50 inches in the southeast. In the winter, the northern parts of the state receive the most snow.

Average Annual Precipitation Across Missouri

There can be great variation in precipitation among the different areas in Missouri. How does location affect the amount of rainfall an area receives?

LEGEND

Average Annual Precipitation (in inches) 1961–1990

200 – 100.1

100 – 25.1

25 – 5 and less

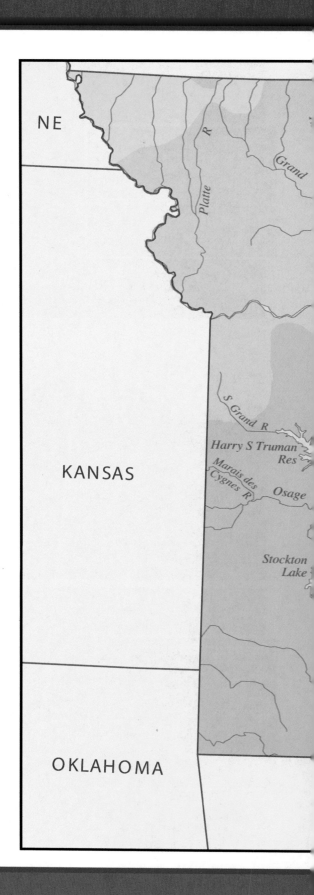

Nature's Resources

Trees cover nearly one-third of Missouri. Oak, walnut, and red cedar trees are found across the state. Forestry is an important business in Missouri, with lumber, flooring, and railroad ties as the key wood products.

The state is also rich in minerals. Missouri has some of the world's largest deposits of lead. Lime, coal, barite, zinc, and iron ore are also mined. Missouri is a leading state in zinc and lime production. Minerals mined in Missouri are sold across the country. Other resources are found in smaller quantities.

Timber brings $3 billion to Missouri's economy each year.

The Missouri and Mississippi Rivers are another important natural resource for the state. Combined, these rivers offer thousands of miles of navigable waterways. Manufactured goods can be moved east and west along the Missouri and south along the Mississippi to the important port city of New Orleans.

The "Lead Belt" in Missouri contains the state's zinc deposits, as well as the world's biggest concentration of lead.

About 5 million tons of cargo move down the Missouri River each year.

Vegetation

Spring is a welcome time in Missouri. Some flowers, such as the spring beauty, bloom as early as the end of February. More than 3,200 species of plants, both native and introduced, grow in Missouri. Among native plants are the Missouri evening primrose, the cream wild indigo, and the Missouri coneflower. Flowers common to the state include violets, buttercups, and wild roses.

Many types of wildflowers line Missouri's roadsides, including Queen Anne's lace, black-eyed Susan, blazing star, and wild sweet William. Wild grape, ivy, and honeysuckle are three of the state's leafy vines. Bluegrass can be found throughout Missouri, although it is not native to the area.

In the 1700s, around one-third of Missouri was covered in prairie grasses. Now, almost all of the land that was once prairie is used as farmland. There are still a number of prairie **reserves** around the state, however.

Wild Columbine

Wild columbine bloom in April and can grow as high as 2 feet. Flowers can be pink, purple, white, yellow, or red. They grow in a variety of soil conditions. They like shade but can also thrive in full sunlight.

Mockernut Hickory

The mockernut hickory is the most common variety of hickory tree. It can live as long as 500 years. Hickory is a hard wood, commonly found in eastern forests.

Violets

Violets are hardy plants that bloom in early spring. They are commonly found in the Ozark Mountains.

Flowering Dogwood

The flowering dogwood rarely grows over 40 feet. It is known for its tiny flowers of four pink or white petals.

Wildlife

About 70 species of mammals live in Missouri's forests and hills. Smaller mammals in the state include rabbits, woodchucks, minks, and opossums. Larger mammals include white-tailed deer, beavers, and coyotes. Black bears and even mountain lions can occasionally be found. Due to hunting and the loss of their natural habitats, some species of animals have disappeared from Missouri. These include the gray wolf, the red wolf, the white-tailed jackrabbit, the Ozark big-eared bat, the elk, and the bison, or buffalo.

For bird-watchers, Missouri is an ideal location. Robins, bluebirds, cardinals, doves, and hawks grace the sky. Bass, pike, perch, and catfish provide good fishing in state waters. Hikers should be careful of venomous rattlesnakes and copperhead snakes that are found in the hills.

Eastern Cottontail Rabbit

Eastern cottontail rabbits live in many areas of Missouri. They have brownish-red coats, slender faces, and a splash of white on the tail. They need good protective cover to survive in the wild.

Channel Catfish

The channel catfish is Missouri's state fish. Although these fish can grow to 45 pounds, this is uncommon in Missouri. Channel catfish are **bottom feeders**, eating insects, mollusks, other fish, and plants.

White-tailed Deer

By 1890, the white-tailed deer was nearly extinct in Missouri. In 1944, deer populations were reported to have increased to about 15,000 because of conservation programs. White-tailed deer are now common throughout Missouri.

Franklin's Ground Squirrel

The Franklin's ground squirrel likes to live in tall grass or mid-grass prairies. It makes its nest in underground burrows. Since its habitat is disappearing, the ground squirrel population is decreasing.

Economy

Johnson's Shut-Ins State Park

Johnson's Shut-Ins State Park is located on the shore of the Taum Sauk Reservoir. A boardwalk provides access to the shut-ins, which are narrow canyons in a wide valley.

Tourism

Missouri's outdoors are a popular destination for vacationers from across the country. The scenic Ozark Mountains are found in the southern part of the state and are shared mostly with Arkansas. The Ozarks offer canyons, caves, and lush forests. The Bagnell Dam on the Osage River has created the Lake of the Ozarks. The lake is the largest **reservoir** in the state. It stretches for 92 miles from one end to the other. Golfing and camping are popular lakeside activities.

Gateway Arch

The Gateway Arch in St. Louis symbolizes the city's role as the Gateway to the West. At 630 feet, the Gateway Arch is the tallest national monument in the country. Visitors can ride to the top to enjoy spectacular views of the city and the Mississippi River.

Hannibal

Fans of American author Samuel Clemens, better known as Mark Twain, will want to visit Hannibal, where he grew up. Visitors can cruise the Mississippi on the Mark Twain Riverboat. During Tom Sawyer Days in July, people enjoy frog jumping contests, mud volleyball, and the National Fence Painting Contest.

Lake of the Ozarks

More than 3 million people visit the Lake of the Ozarks each year. It is the largest lake in Missouri. The lake is a popular destination for wake boarders, water-skiers, swimmers, and boaters.

More than 3,700 people work at the General Motors assembly plant in Wentzville, Missouri.

Primary Industries

Missouri is known as a manufacturing state. More than $30 billion is earned through the sale of manufactured goods every year. Transportation equipment, including cars, trucks, and airplanes, is manufactured in the state. Missouri also has a food-processing industry that produces soft drinks, flour, meats, and canned fruits. Other Missouri-made products include soaps, detergents, missiles, and chemicals for use in farming and medicine.

Kansas City and St. Louis are the major manufacturing centers in Missouri. Kansas City's location near the Great Plains makes it a perfect place for businesses that process agricultural products. In St. Louis, the industries are mostly mechanical. Automobile assembly and aerospace technology make St. Louis a high-technology center.

As of **2012**, **Missouri** had the **second largest** number of farms, after **Texas.**

Every single **Chevrolet Corvette** produced between **1954** and **1981** was made in **St. Louis.**

Value of Goods and Services
(in Millions of Dollars)

Many different industries are important in the state. What evidence allows you to conclude that Missouri's economy is well-balanced?

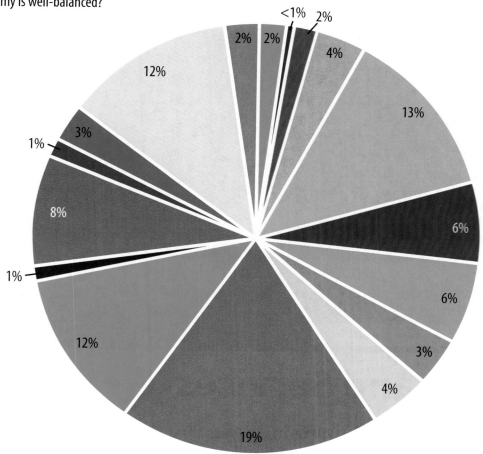

● Agriculture, Forestry, Fishing	$5,573	● Finance, Insurance and Real Estate	$51,977
● Mining	$1,345	● Professional and Business Services	$33,109
● Utilities	$5,377	● Education	$3,258
● Construction	$9,903	● Health Care and Social Assistance	$23,503
● Manufacturing	$34,755	● Arts, Entertainment, and Recreation	$3,760
● Wholesale Trade	$17,531	● Accommodation and Food Services	$7,176
● Retail Trade	$16,853	● Government	$34,068
● Transportation and Warehousing	$9,570	● Other Services	$6,535
● Information	$12,424		

There are about 890 dairy farms in Missouri.

Goods and Services

There are more than 100,000 farms in Missouri. The state is one of the country's leading producers of hay. Other important crops include corn, oats, rice, and tobacco. Cotton, rice, soybeans, sorghum, and wheat grow especially well in southeast Missouri. Soybeans are the state's most valuable crop. In recent years, about 5 million acres of land have been planted with soybeans in Missouri.

In most of the south, the land is too rugged for crops, but it is suitable for raising livestock. The sale of animals and animal products contributes almost $3 billion to Missouri's economy each year. Large livestock farms raise cows and hogs. In some areas, cows and hogs outnumber people. Milk is produced at dairy farms, which are most commonly found in southwestern Missouri. At other farms, chickens are raised for their meat and eggs.

Transportation and aerospace equipment is also produced in the state. The McDonnell Douglas Corporation was known as a major producer of military aircraft and space vehicles. The company's history in Missouri dates back to 1939, when McDonnell Aircraft was founded. In 1997, the company was purchased by the Boeing Company.

Boeing Defense, Space & Security is headquartered in St. Louis, Missouri.

The service sector also contributes greatly to the state's economy. More people work in service jobs than in any other type of employment. Service employees in Missouri work in hotels, restaurants, and stores, among many other places.

Hallmark Cards, Inc. employs about 3,700 people.

History

The Blackfoot lived along the Missouri River. They were thought to be a very strong military power and prevented many fur traders from trapping along the Missouri until the mid-1800s.

Native Americans

The first Native Americans in Missouri are believed to have lived in the area as far back as 12,000 years ago. They were primarily hunter-gatherers. One group, deemed the Clovis culture, most likely hunted mammoths. More than 2,000 years ago, the Woodland cultures came to live in the area. The Missouria people, where the state's name comes from, were one of these Woodland cultures. They raised corn, beans, and squash, and made pottery.

In about 800 AD, the Mound Builders of the Mississippian culture arrived. These people farmed, lived in villages, and were ruled by chiefs who made their headquarters atop large earthen mounds. It is believed that these mounds also served as burial sites and places of worship.

By the 1600s, a number of Native American groups lived in what is now Missouri. The Osage, the Crow, the Blackfoot, and the Sioux settled in villages in the western part of the state. In the east were the Missouri and the Iowa tribes. The area contained bison and other wild animals that were hunted for food. Fish were plentiful in the nearby rivers. Animal skins were used for shelter and clothing.

The Native Americans of Missouri spent about half the year in villages. The other half was spent following migrating bison herds and hunting.

Exploring the Land

The first Europeans to see Missouri were two French explorers, Louis Jolliet and Father Jacques Marquette, who voyaged down the Mississippi River in 1673. In these explorations, the Frenchmen became the first white explorers to come into contact with the Osage, the largest population of Native Americans in the region at the time. In 1682, the entire Mississippi River **drainage basin**, including Missouri, was claimed for France by René-Robert Cavelier, sieur de La Salle.

Timeline of Settlement

European Settlements

1682 René-Robert Cavelier, sieur de La Salle, claims Missouri for France.

1770 The Mission of St. Francis Xavier is established near the site of St. Louis.

1673 Louis Jolliet and Father Jacques Marquette voyage down Mississippi River.

1735 Ste. Genevieve is founded.

1764 St. Louis is founded as a fur-trading post near the confluence of the Missouri and Mississippi Rivers.

Early Exploration

In the years following La Salle's voyage, French fur trappers, fur traders, and **missionaries** moved into the Missouri region. In 1700, the Mission of St. Francis Xavier was established near the site of St. Louis, but it lasted only three years because it had been built on swampy ground. Not long afterward, the French found the Missouri hills to the south to be a valuable source of lead, which they used to make ammunition. However, it was not until about 1735 that Missouri got its first permanent European settlement, at Ste. Genevieve.

Road to Statehood

1812 The U.S. government establishes the Missouri Territory.

1804 The Lewis and Clark Expedition to explore the Louisiana Territory starts in Missouri.

1803 The United States purchases the Louisiana Territory, including Missouri, from France.

1820 Senator Henry Clay of Kentucky proposes the Missouri Compromise, which allows Missouri to enter the Union as a slaveholding state.

U.S. Territory

1821 Missouri becomes the 24th state.

Jacques Marquette was the explorer and missionary who first explored and mapped the northern part of the Mississippi River.

The First Settlers

In 1764, a French fur-trading party led by Pierre Laclède set up a trading post on the west bank of the Mississippi River, just south of where the Missouri flows into it. Only a few months later, the party learned that its new village, which was called St. Louis, sat on territory that France had transferred to Spain. The Spanish made St. Louis the capital of Upper Louisiana.

Spain returned control of the Louisiana Territory to France in 1800, and in 1803, the United States purchased the land. The Lewis and Clark Expedition started out from a base near St. Louis in 1804. By that year, more than 10,000 people were living in Missouri. In the 1820s, steamboats began to navigate on the Mississippi River, making travel and immigration much easier. In 1812, Missouri was organized into a territory by the U.S. government.

The French and the Spanish had allowed slavery in Missouri, and that practice continued. This caused problems in 1818, when Missouri applied to join the Union as a state. The Union was evenly divided between **free states** and **slave states**. Missouri had to wait until a free state, Maine, had been admitted before gaining statehood itself in 1821. The agreement that allowed Maine and Missouri to be admitted was called the Missouri Compromise.

Antoine de Mothe founded St. Philippe on the east side of the Mississippi River. Soon after, he established the first lead mines in Missouri.

Even though slavery was allowed in Missouri, most residents did not want the state to be a part of the **Confederacy** when the Civil War erupted in 1861. Like several other slaveholding states along the border between the North and the South, Missouri stayed in the Union. Most of the fighting that happened in the state was guerrilla warfare along the Kansas-Missouri border and in the Ozark Mountains.

In 1863, Brigadier General Thomas Ewing carried out orders that forcibly removed Missouri residents who had Southern sympathies from their homes.

History Makers

Many notable Missourians have contributed to the development of their state and their country. One even became president of the United States. Other Missourians were political leaders, successful business leaders, made scientific discoveries, and wrote literature that has defined the American experience.

Samuel Clemens "Mark Twain" (1835–1910)

Samuel Clemens was born in Florida, Missouri, and grew up in Hannibal. Clemens used his boyhood memories as material for two of his best-known novels, *Adventures of Tom Sawyer* and *The Adventures of Huckleberry Finn*. His humor, observations of human nature, and use of **dialect** have secured Clemens's place among great American writers.

George Washington Carver (c. 1861–1943)

Born into slavery near Diamond Grove, George Washington Carver became the director of agricultural research at Tuskegee Institute in 1896. There, he developed a variety of products from peanuts and sweet potatoes. Carter's work helped convince southern farmers that it was profitable to grow crops other than cotton.

Scott Joplin (1868–1917)

Scott Joplin is known as the "King of **Ragtime**." He settled in Missouri in 1895. His classic piano rags, such as "The Entertainer" and "The Maple Leaf Rag," had an important impact on the birth of jazz. Interest in Joplin's music revived in the 1970s when it was used in the award-winning score of the film *The Sting*.

Harry S. Truman (1884–1972)

Born in Lamar, Harry Truman became the vice president of the United States in 1944. When President Franklin D. Roosevelt died, Truman became the 33rd president of the United States. He led the country through the end of World War II and the early years of the Cold War.

Misty Copeland (1982–)

Misty Copeland was born in Kansas City, Missouri. She began studying ballet before the age of 13. Through injury and adversity in her home life, Misty continued to dance. In 2015, Copeland became the first African American appointed as an American Ballet Theater principal dancer.

Culture

Kansas City, Missouri, has nearly 500,000 residents. The city is so large it enters into three counties.

Forest Park is one of the largest urban parks in the United States, at 1,293 acres. The park sees about 12 million visitors each year.

The People Today

With a population of almost 6 million in the 2010 Census, Missouri ranked 18th among the states. Its growth rate of 7 percent between 2000 and 2010 was below the average for all states. If the population were evenly spread across Missouri, there would be about 87 people on every square mile of land. Due to the rugged **terrain**, the Ozark region is less populous than the rest of state.

Kansas City is Missouri's largest city by population, but if suburbs are included, the St. Louis metropolitan area is larger. Some of Kansas City's suburbs are in Kansas, and the St. Louis area extends across the Mississippi River into Illinois. Springfield, Independence, and Columbia are the other cities in the state with more than 100,000 people. With a population of slightly more than 40,000, Jefferson City is a small state capital.

Missouri's population has grown steadily but slowly, from just **less than 4 million** in **1950** to almost **6 million** in **2010**.

Q What are some possible reasons why the population has not grown more quickly?

The current capitol building in Jefferson City is the third in the city, but the sixth capitol building in Missouri. It was completed in 1917.

State Government

Missouri has had four constitutions since joining the Union in 1821. The present constitution took effect in 1945. Like the federal government, there are three branches of government in Missouri. They are the executive, the legislative, and the judicial.

Starting in 2013, Missouri will have eight members in the U.S. House of Representatives. Since its population did not grow as much as some other states between 2000 and 2010, Missouri lost one seat in the House of Representatives as a result of the 2010 Census.

The Missouri House of Representatives has 163 members, and the Senate has 34 members. These two chambers make up the state's General Assembly, or legislature, which makes new laws. The Supreme Court of Missouri is the highest court in the state.

Cities and counties play an important role in state politics. Missouri was the first state in the country to allow its cities to have their own home rule **charters**. There are 114 counties in the state, plus St. Louis, which has the status of an independent city.

The interior of the capitol building is covered with several murals. The third floor rotunda features bronze busts of famous Missourians.

Jay Nixon was elected in 2008 as the 55th governor of Missouri.

Missouri's state song is called
"Missouri Waltz."

Hush-a-bye, ma baby, slumbertime is comin' soon;
Rest yo' head upon my breast while Mommy hums a tune;
The sandman is callin' where shadows are fallin',
While the soft breezes sigh as in days long gone by.
Way down in Missouri where I heard this melody,
When I was a little child upon my Mommy's knee;
The old folks were hummin'; their banjos were strummin';
So sweet and low. Strum, strum, strum, strum, strum,
Seems I hear those banjos playin' once again,
Hum, hum, hum, hum, hum, That same old plaintive strain.

*excerpted

The Ozark Folk Festival is the oldest folk festival in the United States. It is nearly 70 years old.

Celebrating Culture

Missouri's rich heritage provides for a wealth of cultural activity. The Ozark region has a strong folk story tradition. Folk music, dancing, food, and crafts are also celebrated in festivals around the state. Homemade funnel cakes are a popular folk snack. Square dancing and clog dancing are performed while musicians play folk instruments. Fiddles, banjos, harmonicas, spoons, and mouth bows combine to create the traditional sounds of folk music. Many music groups play a style of music called **bluegrass**.

European settlers brought their own traditions to Missouri. The large German American population hosts festivals, such as Oktoberfest in the fall, where bratwurst sausage, sauerkraut, and delicate strudel pastries are served. Missouri also has many people of Irish, British, Polish, Greek, and Italian descent.

Although many Native Americans were driven out of Missouri by European settlement, today about 30,000 Native Americans live in Missouri. They honor their traditions at various celebrations. Performers gather around a traditional drum, beating a rhythm. They chant and sing the songs of their ancestors, often wearing traditional clothing and jewelry.

Missouri's rich African American culture is on display in Kansas City in the historic 18th and Vine area. During the early 1900s, this African American neighborhood produced some of the finest jazz ever recorded. Artists such as Count Basie, John Coltrane, and Charlie Parker have helped to make 18th and Vine a location that is known around the world.

The Charlie Parker Memorial sits outside the American Jazz Museum in Kansas City. It was dedicated on March 27, 1999.

In recent years, the Hispanic and Asian populations of Missouri have been growing. Most members of these groups live in and around Missouri's large cities. Some have moved to southwestern Missouri to work in the state's lucrative poultry industry.

The Japanese Festival in the Missouri Botanical Gardens is one of the largest and oldest celebrations of Japanese heritage in the United States.

Born in St. Louis, Missouri, Chuck Berry is considered one of the pioneers of rock and roll music.

Arts and Entertainment

As jazz music made its way up the Mississippi River from New Orleans, St. Louis became an important station along the way. Kansas City, however, is better known as a jazz center. Such greats as saxophonists Lester Young and Charlie Parker, and bandleader Count Basie were part of the local scene. A little later, St. Louis became a center for rhythm and blues, the place where Chuck Berry and Ike and Tina Turner made their reputations.

Missouri has produced many motion picture giants as well. Walt Disney grew up in Marceline and St. Louis. Director Robert Altman, known for such TV shows as *M*A*S*H*, *Nashville*, and *The Player*, was born in Kansas City. Actors Jon Hamm, Kevin Kline, and Kathleen Turner all come from Missouri.

The first college-level **journalism class** in the world was taught at the University of Missouri, Columbia, in 1879.

Missouri is **home** to the **second oldest civic orchestra** in the **U.S.**

Missouri has produced many talented writers. The poets T. S. Eliot, Langston Hughes, and Sara Teasdale were all born in Missouri. Eliot is considered one of the greatest poets of the twentieth century, and most people think he had the Mississippi in mind when he wrote in a poem that "the river is a strong brown god." Laura Ingalls Wilder also lived in Missouri. She wrote many of the popular *Little House* books at her family home in the Ozarks.

In recent years, the Ozark Mountain town of Branson has become a major center for live entertainment. More than 40 theaters offer a wide variety of shows, mostly musicals, performed by well-known entertainers. Beginning in the 1980s, country music stars from Nashville, Tennessee, began establishing large venues to play, making Branson a must-see destination for country music fans.

T.S. Eliot was born in St. Louis, Missouri, in 1888.

Jazz festivals are common in Missouri. They happen throughout the year and in every major city in the state.

The Upper Missouri River National Monument is a common area to experience the outdoor recreation available in Missouri.

Sports and Recreation

Missourians, young and old, love sports. The state has a total of five major league sports teams. Baseball enthusiasts follow the St. Louis Cardinals and the Kansas City Royals. The St. Louis Rams and the Kansas City Chiefs play in the National Football League. In winter, the St. Louis Blues hockey team hits the ice. The team was named in honor of a musical composition by W. C. Handy.

Missouri is also the site of several sports museums. In 1991, the Negro Leagues Baseball Museum opened in Kansas City. The museum celebrates the history of African American baseball. St. Louis, the home of several bowling champions, houses the International Bowling Museum & Hall of Fame. The Missouri Sports Hall of Fame is in Springfield.

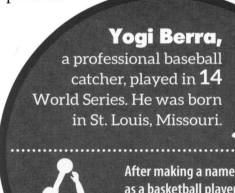

Yogi Berra, a professional baseball catcher, played in **14** World Series. He was born in St. Louis, Missouri.

After making a name for himself as a basketball player, Missouri-born **BILL BRADLEY** later went on to become a U.S. senator, and even ran for president in 1999.

Outdoor sports are popular in Missouri. The state's rivers are ideal for canoeing and rafting, and cyclists can cover the 200-mile-long Katy Trail. With more than 6,300 caves in the state, **spelunking** is another favorite activity. Some of the more popular caves include Meramec Caverns, hideout of the outlaw Jesse James, and the Mark Twain Cave near Hannibal, where a well-known episode in the TV adaptation of Mark Twain's *The Adventures of Tom Sawyer* was set.

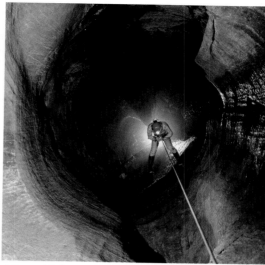

Missouri is known as "The Cave State," and spelunking is a popular activity for tourists and locals. New caves are being formed in the Ozarks even today.

Fishing and hunting are common pursuits in Missouri's many lakes, rivers, and forests. Game hunters seek out quail, pheasant, wild turkey, rabbit, and deer. Fishers catch bass, catfish, bluegill, and jack salmon. Float fishing is common in the Ozarks. Float fishers travel down rivers and around lakes, trailing fishing line behind them.

In 2015, the Kansas City Royals beat the New York Mets to win the World Series.

Get To Know
MISSOURI

ICED TEA

was invented at the Missouri World's Fair in 1904.

COVERING **93** SQUARE MILES, **the Lake of the Ozarks** IS ONE OF THE LARGEST MAN-MADE LAKES IN THE UNITED STATES.

SITTING IN THE MIDDLE OF **"TORNADO ALLEY,"** MISSOURI SEES, ON AVERAGE, **25** TORNADOES PER YEAR.

Kansas City, Missouri has more **fountains** than any other city in the world except Rome.

The world's largest **ball of nylon twine,** at more than **13 feet tall** and **13,000 pounds,** can be seen in Branson, Missouri.

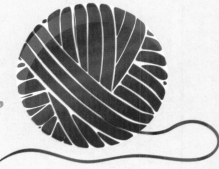

In the skies of St. Louis, the first-ever successful sky dive from an airplane was completed in 1912 by **Captain Berry.**

The southeastern area of Missouri, following along the Mississippi River, is fondly called the "**Bootheel**" thanks to its shape.

Brain Teasers

What have you learned about Missouri after reading this book? Test your knowledge by answering these questions. All of the information can be found in the text you just read. The answers are provided below for easy reference.

1 What is the capital of Missouri?

2 Where could pioneers catch the Santa Fe and Oregon Trails out west?

3 What is the highest point in Missouri?

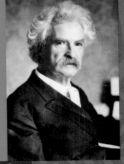

4 What pen name did famous writer Samuel Clemens choose for himself?

5 What caused the severe earthquakes of 1811 and 1812 in Missouri?

6 How many plant species grow in Missouri?

7

What is the tallest national monument in the country?

8 Which United States president was born in Lamar, Missouri?

Key Words

bluegrass: a style of hard-driving country music featuring the banjo

bottom feeders: aquatic animals that feed at the bottom of a body of water

charters: documents that set out the rights of an organization or a group

Confederacy: the southern states that opposed the Union in the Civil War

confluence: the place where two or more rivers join

dialect: speech that is characteristic of a certain region

drainage basin: the area drained by a river

fertile: rich in the nutrients required to grow crops

free states: states that did not permit slavery

missionaries: people traveling to promote religion in a foreign country

ragtime: a type of music played mainly on the piano, developed from African American folk music

reserves: protected areas for nature

reservoir: artificially created body of water

slave states: states that permitted slavery

spelunking: exploring caves and underground caverns

terrain: land

Index

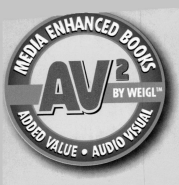

Log on to www.av2books.com

AV² by Weigl brings you media enhanced books that support active learning. Go to www.av2books.com, and enter the special code found on page 2 of this book. You will gain access to enriched and enhanced content that supplements and complements this book. Content includes video, audio, weblinks, quizzes, a slide show, and activities.

AV² Online Navigation

Audio
Listen to sections of the book read aloud

Book Pages
AV² pages directly correspond to pages in the book.

Video
Watch informative video clips.

Key Words
Study vocabulary, and complete a matching word activity.

Embedded Weblinks
Gain additional information for research.

Try This!
Complete activities and hands-on experiments.

Quizzes
Test your knowledge.

Slide Show
View images and captions, and prepare a presentation.

AV² was built to bridge the gap between print and digital. We encourage you to tell us what you like and what you want to see in the future.

Sign up to be an AV² Ambassador at www.av2books.com/ambassador.